Welcome to a
Life of Faith
in the Episcopal Church

Welcome to a Life of Faith in the Episcopal Church

Megan Castellan

CHURCH
PUBLISHING
INCORPORATED

Church Publishing
19 East 34th Street
New York, NY 10016
www.churchpublishing.org

Typeset by Denise Hoff

A record of this book is available from the Library of Congress.
ISBN-13: 978-1-64065-136-4 (pbk.)
ISBN-13: 978-1-64065-137-1 (ebook)

Contents

Introduction

Perhaps it was an internet search. Perhaps it was a friend's wedding. Perhaps it was the way the building looked in the sunlight—all bright and shiny. Perhaps it was the children's programs they offered, or the food pantry that opens in the evenings, or the welcome preaching, or the promise of a safe space to land and rest.

Whatever the reason, you have found your way into an Episcopal church—welcome!

In some ways, the Episcopal Church is a well-kept secret. The name is a tongue twister; a Greek word that is rarely heard and frequently confounding. Episcopal churches rarely splash across the headlines for their enormity or their wealth. Episcopalians have never been the majority denomination in the United States, and we are hardly likely to start now.

But in other ways, Episcopalians have always been woven into the fabric of this nation. Though they may not advertise it, Episcopal churches sit on corners throughout the United States and around the world. The prayers we say each day and the faith we proclaim have shaped the lives of countless people throughout history. In subtle ways, Episcopalians have been walking unseen in the footsteps of Jesus for a long time.

If you were curious enough to pick up this book in an attempt to find out more, let me encourage you to reach out to your local parish. You don't have to say anything smart or clever; you don't have to have fully formed questions or know the lingo. But as you'll find in these pages, the journey of faith is never taken alone. And I trust and pray that the God who has led you this far has made a place for you where that journey may continue.

May every blessing rise to meet you on your path, and may the Spirit guide you into all truth.

The Faith
We Proclaim:
The Bible

One of the bits of kitchen-table wisdom Episcopalians toss around is that we enjoy the Bible because it reminds us so much of the Book of Common Prayer.

That's a well-worn joke, yet the fact remains that the prayer book borrows almost 75 percent of its language from the Bible. The Bible contributed its phrases, its laments, and its words of triumph to the prayers and praises of our lit-

Liturgy is a Greek word that literally means "the work done on behalf of the people." We will unpack what exactly that means a bit later, but for now, know that a church liturgy is a set series of prayers, scripture readings, and actions.

urgy, and we come to know the scriptures in part as we absorb the words of our common prayer.

That fact alone indicates how important the Bible has been to Anglicans through the centuries. Miles Coverdale, one of the first English translators of the Bible, was so respected by Thomas Cranmer, that the Coverdale translation of the Psalms was included in the 1549 Book of Common Prayer, and his basic translation has remained at the heart of our prayer book psalms ever since. (That's why they sound different than the psalms in your Bible on the shelf.) Cranmer saw the Book of Common Prayer as a way to facilitate and guide the reading of the Bible by the masses in England, once the Bible was readily available in English—which was also why he included tools like a daily lectionary,

A lectionary is a prescribed schedule of readings from the Bible over a given period of time.

and a three-year eucharistic lectionary. The prayer book and Bible were always intended to work together.

WHY IS THE BIBLE SO IMPORTANT FOR CHRISTIANS?

As Christians, we read the Bible constantly. The Bible is read at all public and private liturgies. The words of scripture inform every action that we take.

Simply put, we believe the Bible contains profound truth about humanity's ongoing relationship with God. For this reason, we try to incorporate the Bible into much of our daily life and practice.

Invoking the claim of truth regarding the Bible is a tricky thing. For some, it may conjure up images of doomsday preachers trying to parse out the lottery numbers by reading their Bible the right way, or arguing against evolution. However, I mean something very different; when I assert the Bible is true, I am claiming the same sort of truth that one would recognize in a great work of art; truth that bypasses the literal meaning and resonates in the soul.

The catechism, in the back of the prayer book, says it this way: "We believe the Old and New Testaments to be the Word of God, and contain all things necessary to salvation."[1] That's a

---

1 BCP, p. 868.

uniquely Anglican turn of phrase and deserves some unpacking.

Word of God

When Episcopalians say this, we are indicating that the Bible conveys vital information about God and God's nature to us in a particular way. We regard the Bible as different from all other books because we believe that the Holy Spirit speaks to us through its words, and that over time, it continues to reveal to us the nature of God's will for God's people.

In other words, the Bible remains affected by its cultural context, the way it was written, and how we interpret it, but still we believe that the truth in it remains relevant to our lives as people seeking a relationship to God today in the twenty-first century.

Contains All Things Necessary for Salvation

This phrase comes from a statement called the *Thirty-Nine Articles*: a document compiled during Elizabeth I's reign in England as an attempt to codify what the Anglican Church believed. The writers tried to create a common ground between Roman Catholics, who were still grieving the loss of the pope's authority in England, and the Puritans, who thought the English Reformation hadn't gone far enough.

On the subject of scripture, the Catholics wanted biblical authority to be taken only with the church's teaching, reasoning that individuals couldn't be trusted to read the Bible on their own without guidance. After all, the people were mostly uneducated and illiterate, and there was original sin to take into account. There's a lot of odd stuff in the Bible—who knows what crazy ideas the common person could invent for themselves?

The Puritans, by contrast, wanted the church to announce that salvation could be found only through reading the Bible, and the faith that such reading inspired. Sure, they pointed out, most people couldn't read, but how better to teach them through the words of the holiest of books? Why cut people off from the most profound source of truth there was?

The Anglican Church found a compromise and announced that *"the scriptures contained all things necessary to salvation."*[2] That is, you did

---

2 "Article VI. Of the Sufficiency of the Holy Scriptures for Salvation," BCP, p. 868.

not need a pope to give you additional wisdom, but neither were you required to profess specific scriptural truths in order to win salvation. Basically, it's a lengthy way of saying that all we need to know about God is in the Bible somewhere . . . but *where exactly* it is can be debated. If you grew up in a tradition that saw the Bible as containing an exact series of beliefs that you must endorse to be saved, then this might seem like a big change!

That being said, the Episcopal Church does approach the Bible differently than some other Christian churches.

While Episcopalians do believe the Bible is the Word of God, and we regard it very highly, there is a sizeable difference between the Anglican stance, and the approach of many current American denominations.[3] Like the divide that the Thirty-Nine Articles tried to bridge, there are many ways of approaching the Bible, and you may be accustomed to another approach. Truth is

---

3 It's worth noting that the idea of literal interpretation of the Bible is very modern, and very American. It was first enshrined in the American consciousness in the early 1900s, as part of the five Christian fundamentals espoused by the rallying conservative denominations. Worldwide, and from a historical perspective, this approach to biblical study is both a novelty and an aberration.

multivalent and multivocal—and even when we all accept something as truth, faithful people can disagree about what, exactly, we are accepting. Especially when engaging with truth as powerful and as complicated as the Bible, it makes sense that Christians, throughout history, would try many different methods to understand.

Some churches believe in a doctrine called "verbal inerrancy." This concept means that the people who wrote the Bible were so inspired by God that literally every word of what we term *scripture* is literally, factually, correct. Frequently, this belief causes these churches to have very strict rules about which translations of the scriptures they use.

The Episcopal Church does not hold to this doctrine. Instead, the Episcopal Church has historically believed that the Bible must be understood by humans reading in community with our common sense and reason fully engaged. We understand that the Bible was written in particular time periods, in particular cultural contexts, by particular human beings, who were as flawed as anyone else. The Bible we now read is a result of translations from Hebrew and Greek, cobbled together piecemeal from many manuscripts

written over many centuries, and read through
the lenses of our own time and place—and because of these things, our interpretations of any
given scripture will vary: both over time, and
from person to person.

That variance is a good thing. It reminds us
that the truth of God remains a mystery that we
only know a small part of. It also requires us to
rely on one another. Someone else will have a
different perspective on a passage that I struggle with, and their insight might be just what I
need to hear. I might see something in a verse because of my particular experience that someone
else doesn't see. We might come to loggerheads
over a story that remains unclear, which indicates
that we need to stay in conversation longer. But
at every turn, the complexity of scripture requires
humility and a group effort. No one can untangle
God's word alone—we need each other.

So then, the Episcopal Church does not read
the Bible literally. Passages like the description
of a seven-day creation in Genesis, or Joshua
making the sun stand still in Numbers, are not
taken as historical fact, the way we might read
a newspaper report. Neither are Paul's prohibi-
tions against women speaking publicly in church

in 1 Corinthians seen as binding for all time and all places.

Rather, in keeping with the other information we have learned about the Bible over time—both from academic scholars and religious leaders—we know that the Bible contains many genres of writing. Some stories were meant to explain the mythic origins and purpose of creation. Other parts, like Paul's letters, were instructions to a particular community on a particular subject. If our aim is to hear the Spirit speaking to us through the words of scripture, we can only do that if we take into account everything we know about the scripture—and that includes its context. To read the Bible literally would be to degrade its value and meaning. It would be like cherishing your iPhone because it functioned as a serviceable doorstop! Sure, it works; but it's a mere glimpse of everything it could do and be.

As an example, consider the opening chapter of Genesis. It's famous; you probably are familiar with it. "In the beginning . . . God created the heavens and the earth. . . . And there was evening and there was morning, the first day." Creation continues in a predictable pattern, as God creates the sun, moon, stars, oceans, aquatic and land animals, and finally, humans. God declares it all good, then takes a day of rest.

It's a lovely story.

Then, however, if you are reading along, you continue to the next verse only to discover that the entire story *starts over again*. No sooner has God rested on the newly created Sabbath, then the narrative is back to describing the earth as a formless, dry void, and God again creates life— only in the *opposite* order as in the first story. If you read carefully, you can discern that Genesis 1 is the opposite of Genesis 2. Genesis 1 is orderly, almost rhythmic, in its precision of language. God creates and declares creation good. Humanity is the icing on the cake. In Genesis 2, God creates humans first, then spends the rest of creation trying to find the ur-Man a partner.[4] Man has the happy task of naming the other newly formed creations as God creates them.

If one were to take this literally, one would have to believe that God initially created all that

---

4 And here's another difference, which comes through in some English translations, like the New Revised Standard Version: In Genesis 1, the term is *humanity*; and in Genesis 2, the term is "man." There are complicated linguistic reasons for this, but just know that it's because it's a literal different word in the Hebrew text.

was in a seven-day period, then undid it in a blinding flash of light only to reengineer the entire creation process so that humanity could participate in it. That is a fairly convoluted cosmology, to say the least.[5]

If you did not want to take those two chapters literally, instead you could examine their context. According to scholarly consensus, we know that those two chapters were written at different times, by different scribes—then were edited together at a much later date. Genesis 1, with its precision and liturgical approach to creation, was written by the Israelite priestly class during a time of exile and religious persecution by the Babylonians. Genesis 2, with its concern about humans and our role in creation, was written earlier, perhaps during the time of King David, and a united Israelite kingdom.

Genesis 1's story, with its order, precision, and ritual, reflects the ritual of temple worship. It shows the almighty God of creation engaging in the same routines that humans engage in when they worship—implying that the rituals that the Jewish peo-

---

5 It also raises some troubling theological questions (i.e., where did all the first round of animals go? Was God lying when God indicated they were good, etc.?).

ple engaged in when they went to the temple were intimately tied to the Divine itself. It also specifically pushes back on the beliefs of some surrounding cultures. Babylonians, for example, believed that humans were created as an afterthought during a war between the gods, and were then made to be slaves for them. Genesis 1 takes pains to show humanity as intentional, reflective of God's very being, and working with God to care for creation, rather than as a lowly servant. Humans, and God, even get a day off for rest—such is how highly prized humanity is in this cosmology![6]

Genesis 2, on the other hand, is more convoluted. God is not quite all-powerful; in fact, God repeatedly fails to create a helper for Adam and cannot even name his animals! Instead, this story seems to emphasize the need for humans to live in community with one another, as most of the story centers around Adam's search for a companion among God's other creatures.

It also hammers home the idea of equality between genders. Importantly, Eve becomes to

---

6 Cosmology is the study of the origin, evolution, and fate of the world. In a religious context, it describes what people believe about where they come from and what their purpose ultimately is.

Adam an equal partner and helper, rather than a subordinate. He greets her as an equal, as compared to the animals and lower beings he has been dealing with to that point (and as compared to the punishment that ensues for her following the apple-eating incident). Genesis 2 is an entirely different story from Genesis 1.

Once you know that context, and can appreciate these stories for what they are, the stories of creation are no longer just about how the earth was made. Now those stories speak about how we relate to one another, how genders relate to each other, what we believe about rest and work, and a whole multitude of other issues that are present in our lives now. Reading the Bible in this way enlivens it and makes it fully active and real for us.

The Faith We Proclaim: Beliefs

THEOLOGY

For avid baseball fans, a good game creates a whole world. The world of baseball has rules, expectations, and specific terms. People acquainted with this world know how it works and can explain it to others. They know what they're looking at when they watch a game, and everyone agrees on the meaning of events as they occur. Player hits the ball? He should run! Player catches the ball in the air? Batter is now out. A web of meaning is created and shared.

As Christians, we also live within a web of meaning. We have language, beliefs, and ideas about the world we inhabit. We have expectations about the way this world functions and how we conduct ourselves within it. This web of meaning is called *theology*. No one web of meaning is exclusive; each of us have a few different webs from which we construct our beliefs. You may see the world through the webs of American civil religion, Protestantism, and bits of capitalism; I may see it through nationalism and Catholicism.

The word *theology* literally means the study of God, or the study of how a world works with God in it. To study God is somewhat of a contradiction in terms—as hard as we might try, we cannot ever really figure out God. But the discipline of theology encourages us to come up with language for God and our faith that other people can understand. Theology is less about trying to nail down God and more about sharing our experience with God.

> To study God is somewhat of a contradiction in terms–as hard as we might try, we cannot ever really figure out God.

We start by agreeing on some common language— words we can all use to signify specific ideas and experiences. For the Episcopal Church, this begins with the Nicene Creed.

NICENE CREED

The Nicene Creed is a statement written very early in the life of the church. The emperor Constantine, after converting to Christianity, convened several meetings of church leaders, which culminated in the creed. Prior to these meetings, or ecumenical councils, Christianity had been underground, and highly localized.[7] People in one part of the Roman Empire could believe something radically different from people in another part. Constantine wanted some standards and agreement in the basics of Christianity across his realm if he was going to make this the official imperial religion. Rome wasn't about to get on board with an uncontrollable religion that couldn't even get its leaders to agree on what Christianity was. Therefore, Constantine got all the leaders together at the Council of Nicea in 325 CE. What emerged from that

---

7 An ecumenical council here refers to a meeting of all the church leaders in the world. (Literally. Because the church was small, this could be done back in the day.) There were seven altogether. (Or four, if you ask the Eastern Orthodox, and eleven if you ask the Roman Catholics.)

meeting was the outline of the Nicene Creed—though it wouldn't take final shape until roughly a hundred years later.

A creed is a statement of belief recited together by the gathered congregation. It comes from the Latin word credo, meaning "to trust in."

The creed was one of the first work products of a church committee. This is important to remember when we read it today, as it is notable both for what it says and what it avoids saying. The Nicene Creed takes pains to say that Jesus Christ and God the Father are of the same substance—a highly specific claim for people in the fourth century, but largely unilluminating for those of us in the twenty-first century. However, it makes no claims as to some other issues, like who goes to heaven, or who should be ordained.

What the creed was designed to do was *not* to lay out specific elements all Christians must believe, or else. Instead, it was an attempt to mark the boundaries for what was acceptable and unacceptable. The Nicene Creed, unlike many more modern statements of faith, is remarkably flexible. It was the guardrails on a highway, intended to keep the faithful on the road and away from dragons living in the ditches.

This expansiveness is also why we recite the creed together as a prayer. On any given day, at any given moment, it is probable that people in a congregation have differing interpretations of what it means. One person may believe devoutly in a bodily resurrection; one person may think it is more of a spiritual experience. One person may be struggling with the idea of forgiveness that day, and one person could be struggling with the idea of an afterlife. But we all join together and pray these words, because the creed reflects the patchwork of our collective experiences. It is always a communal statement that we individually aspire to. Indeed, the word *credo* is Latin for "to trust in"—which indicates that when we recite the creed, we aren't proclaiming facts of which we are intellectually convinced; we are describing ideas in which we hope. We hope in the apostolic church, we rely in one baptism for the forgiveness of sins, etc. As much as the creed outlines our world, it also outlines where and in whom we place our hopes.

Or, to phrase it another way: the creed tells a story about the sort of world we inhabit and the sort of people we try to be. The creed can be a lens through which we see the world—a lens that tells us that God's love and goodness reign supreme, and that God is always working to redeem this messy and half-finished creation through Jesus. Our reciting of the story is our way of assenting to being an active part of the story's unfolding. Reciting the creed is our agreement to seeing the world and living in the world as though these things are profoundly true.

THE BASICS

The Episcopal Church shares the basics of the Christian faith with the rest of global Christianity. We too trust in this story laid out in the creeds: that God—the divine creator of all that is—chose to become human in the person of Jesus of Nazareth, who lived as we do. Jesus's life ended at the hands of the Roman Empire, and yet God raised him from the dead after three days. Through this miraculous series of events, we have come to know the full extent of God's love for creation, and we now know that sin and death no longer have the final word. Now, we try to live our lives in such a way that these truths are proclaimed in everything that we do, until such a time when all creation is finally set free by God's love.

All Christians share the same basic story, and we all share the same basic ideas about what the story means. However, different churches have, over time, emphasized different parts of the story as they grew in their own context.

For Anglicans, the Incarnation has always been particularly important within the story of Jesus. The idea that God became human, in a particular time, in a particular place, in a particular set of circumstances, has inspired Anglican thought for a long time. It is, of course, not entirely new. Irenaeus, the second-century bishop of Lyons, noted that God became human so that humans could become fully divine. But Anglicans took particular joy in the notion that there was something so indelibly loveable about humanity and the material world that God longed to be one of us. Over time, this reverence for the Incarnation has shown itself in various ways. It has fostered a care for liturgical beauty, and for the fine arts and music. It has encouraged some of the world's greatest artists, like C. S. Lewis and Madeleine L'Engle. Perhaps most stirringly, it has led to some of the social justice movements that have shaped our world, like the abolition of slavery, led by William Wilberforce, and the creation of the modern welfare state, led in Great Britain by William Temple and in the United States by Frances Perkins.

Anglicans took particular joy in the notion that there was something so indelibly loveable about humanity and the material world that God longed to be one of us.

This is not to suggest that Anglican theology eliminates the concept of sin or the need for repentance. Indeed, it would be impossible to love the human world as dearly as Anglican theology does without recognizing and struggling with its troubled state. Instead, Anglican theology, at its best, tries to center on people and the world Christ died to redeem, rather than disembodied ideas. A good Anglican theologian tries to find the scripture and words to describe how the Spirit is present in the people and circumstances around her, rather than to change the people to fit "what the Bible says." That human-centered approach is perhaps the greatest contribution Anglican theology has given to the wider Christian world.

Far from being a relativistic, diluted approach, this Anglican way of seeing the world is borne of a deep faith that the God who became human in Jesus, the poor Palestinian Jewish rabbi, will always address the needs of God's human children, whatever they may be. God was not content to leave us in our brokenness and came to dwell in our midst in a particular way, in a particular context. When we seek to apply the teachings of Christ and the precepts of the gospel to this new age, to observe the Spirit present in our time and place, we are bearing witness to this profound and transformative incarnational faith.

THE BOOK OF COMMON PRAYER

If you find yourself sitting in an Episcopal Church in the United States, you will most likely find two books sitting in the pews: a blue book with *Hymnal 1982* printed on the cover and a red book with a gold cross on the cover. That red book is the Book of Common Prayer—the common element binding the Anglican tradition together since its inception in the sixteenth century.[8]

The prayer book in use currently in The Episcopal Church hails from 1979. Some parishes

---

8 Red is the most popular color for pew BCPs in English by my estimation. However, the Spanish-language BCP is frequently found in blue, and occasionally, one may chance upon a hardcover prayer book in another color. No theological conclusion can be drawn from this; God cherishes all prayer books equally, regardless of color.

have permission still to use the earlier book, written in 1928, but these are few and far between.

The current edition was a total renovation of the liturgy, focusing the life of the church on two central points: baptism and the Eucharist. All worship, and therefore theology, flows forth from these two pivotal moments. Baptism calls us into community together with each other and with God, as well as tells us what it means to live a Christian life. Eucharist is the weekly enactment, in word and deed, of what a Christ-shaped life looks like, when lived according to our baptismal vows, as the gathered community meets, hears the Word of God, blesses the gifts we receive, shares them, and goes back into the world, renewed to do Christ's work. In the Eucharist, we regularly encounter Christ, so that we may continually serve the world in Christ's name.

Many resources can be found within the book. There are the resources for corporate, public worship that govern our common life, of course. These include the rites for all the public services of the church: baptism, marriage, ordination, Eucharist, burial. When you attend worship at an Episcopal Church, the words to pray are usually found in the prayer book.

However, the prayer book also contains much more than that. It contains a calendar of days to sanctify how we experience time. Right off the bat, the calendar reframes how we understand the passage of time and places it in a context of liturgy. So if you follow the prayer book, you don't just mark the coming of spring and the brightening of the days, you observe Lent and the events of Holy Week, as Jesus dies and is resurrected again on Easter. The year now echoes the rhythms of the Incarnation.

Next in the book is the Daily Office, a series of set prayers that are based on the daily cycle said by monastics. More will be said about the Office in another place, but note here that there are several options given for the whole thing: one in older, "thee/thou" language, one in more modern language, and a shortened version intended for busy individuals or families pressed for time. It should be noted that one of the major advances that the Book of Common Prayer made was giving the average churchgoer access to all the liturgies of the church. When Thomas Cranmer wrote the first book in the 1550s, he handed access to the rites and rituals, which had previously been reserved only to the ordained clergy, to vowed monastics living in cloisters. Now, if people have this book, they have all they need.

Following the Daily Office, the Great Litany appears, along with the collects for various times and seasons, in both traditional and modern language. A *litany* is a form of prayer that takes the shape of a list or a series of petitions and responses, that alternate between the leader and the congregation. The Litany is one of the first pieces of liturgy written by Cranmer and springs from a medieval tradition of saints' litanies and litanies dedicated to particular community needs. Here, Cranmer essentially combines all the litanies in use at the time, removes the emphasis on the saints, and condenses it for general use. Today, the litany is mostly recited at the beginning of the service at the beginning of Advent and the beginning of Lent. It may also be used in times of national anxiety, or peril, along with the Supplication.

After the collects, we move on to services for special days. Here, we find the special services appointed for Ash Wednesday, Palm Sunday, Maundy Thursday, Good Friday, and the Easter Vigil. Notably, the service of Holy Baptism is within the Easter Vigil service, so whenever a baptism is performed, even if it is in the dead of winter, liturgically, according to the prayer book, you are in the midst of Easter!

From there, the services move in the order of life: after baptism comes the services of the Eucharist, which probably feature well-worn pages that fall open easily, if you are thumbing through a pew copy. The service of the Eucharist follows a general pattern that has been practiced in the church since the first century, and we will discuss this more extensively in a later chapter. The expectation of this prayer book is that Eucharist occurs in every church every week. Along with baptism, it is the most important sacrament, and the foundation upon which everything else rests.

After the Eucharist services comes confirmation. This represents a slight change in approach from earlier books. Previously, children had to be confirmed in order to receive communion, but because of the greater understanding of baptism as complete entry into the body of Christ, that is no longer the case today. Confirmation, instead, is an adult affirmation of the promises made at baptism, and the chance to join the wider expression of the church by being received by the bishop.

Other stages-of-life services also appear: marriage, ordination to the different orders of ministry, thanksgiving for a child, burial, and reconciliation of a penitent. Unlike in other churches, in the Episcopal Church, the rite of reconciliation is not mandatory, but is available, and you may find it helpful if you are struggling particularly with guilt or shame over some situation.

The second half of the prayer book is almost entirely dedicated to the Psalter, or the book of Psalms. All of the one hundred and fifty psalms are printed in the prayer book for ease of reference and use in praying. For centuries, the Psalter has been integral to the prayers of the church, containing the whole range of human emotions imaginable, from lament, to rage, to joy. The Daily Office lectionary, if followed, will let you read all one hundred and fifty psalms in the course of seven weeks. There are also demarcations in the Psalter itself that mark the traditional Anglican divisions, so that if you wanted, you could read all one hundred and fifty over the course of a single month.

You may notice that the translation in the prayer book is different than that in your Bible. This is because the Prayer Book Psalter is based on Miles Coverdale's translation (remember him?), but has been extensively updated since the seventeenth century, as knowledge and scholarship of ancient Hebrew has improved. The current Psalter has been translated with an eye toward Coverdale's poetry of language, for ease of singing and setting to music, and attentiveness to accurate meaning. Because the psalms are poetry, all efforts have been made to render them into similarly beautiful and rhythmic language here.

Alongside the varieties of experiences expressed in the psalms, the prayer book also includes a variety of concerns expressed in prayers and thanksgivings. No matter what you struggle with, chances are there is a prayer here addressing it. There are prayers for human unity, for sound government, for rural areas, for seasonable weather, for the lonely, etc. Like the psalms, the multitude of prayers here reflect the reality that people have struggled with the same things we struggle with and have given us language to make those struggles known to God.

The prayer book gives us a language to frame our talk with God. It gives us a path to walk on our daily journey of faith. Rather than giving us a prescription of what that talk should be or what direction to take, it gives us options and ways that our ancestors have used before us. It puts into our hands the full resources of our tradition, so that no matter what happens, we can find words to speak to God.

SACRAMENTS

Christianity has been an embodied faith right from the start—at times, uncomfortably so. The revelation of God-in-Christ and the resurrection from the dead made clear to the first Christians that this physical world could not be ignored or discounted, but was an intentional and beloved part of God's plan. They went to some rather unusual lengths to illustrate that. Ancient Roman texts suggest that early Christians were known for meeting in graveyards and holding dinner parties in the catacombs. This struck non-Christian Romans as creepy and unsavory. The Christians just thought they were living into Christ's power over death in a concrete way.

Sacraments rose out of this concern with the material world. In sacraments, we have breadcrumbs of God's involvement and presence with us in specific and material ways. The Episcopal catechism defines a sacrament as "an outward and visible sign of an inward and spiritual grace."[9] This definition indicates that a sacrament is some signal whereby other people can see in concrete terms what God has done for a person on a spiritual level. It's a way of making the invisible, visible—through word, action, or ritual.

There are seven sacraments recognized by the Episcopal Church: the two instituted by Jesus Christ himself during his lifetime, and the five practiced through history by the Church. The two sacraments that most people encounter on a regular basis are baptism and Eucharist—the two Jesus interacted with in the Gospels.

Baptism

Baptism is the ancient rite of initiation into the church. Remarkably, the rite we know as Episcopalians is fairly similar to what scholars think it looked like two thousand years ago. Baptism emerged from the Jewish practice of ritual washing, but took on added significance within the new Christian communities. Instead of just cleansing away both physical and spiritual impurities, now the water came to represent death

---

9 BCP, p. 857.

itself, as the baptized person is born into life in Christ. Baptistries (that is, pools where baptisms can take place) are found in the ruins of the oldest churches in the world, so this sacrament has always been a part of church practice.

Today, the ritual of baptism looks much the same. The baptized person is asked to renounce Satan, and all wickedness that corrupts the creatures of God, and to accept Jesus Christ as Lord and Savior. There are three renunciations and three affirmations, which balance each other out. In ancient times, the candidate for baptism would actually physically turn away as s/he renounced evil, and turn toward the east, and the hope of new life, as they accepted Christ. To seal this change, the community then joins with the candidate and affirms the Baptismal Covenant together.

One of the hallmarks of baptism in the Episcopal tradition is that it is public. While formerly, private baptisms were not uncommon, today our understanding is that baptism not only gives new life in Christ, but that new life joins you to Christ's body. Therefore, the local parish, as the physical manifestation of Christ's body, is present to witness and rejoice with the newly baptized.

We'll note here that the Episcopal Church practices infant baptism as well. While there are certainly strong arguments in favor of adult baptism (or "believer's baptism"), Episcopalians continue to welcome children into the church. In a real sense, infant baptism is an expression of God's grace, as it is not through our own action or understanding that we are saved, but only through God's work of redemption. When we welcome babies into the church through baptism, it is a recognition that we don't choose the life of faith—it chooses us.

The Baptismal Covenant is also a hallmark of our Episcopal tradition. It is a series of questions and answers that lay out how the church understands what it takes to live a faithful life in Christ. The first part of it is simply the Apostles' Creed—a summary of the Nicene Creed—in which the community testifies to its faith in God as the Creator, the Christ, and the Spirit at work in our midst. Then the covenant continues with a series of questions that lay out how we intend to make those beliefs real in our daily lives.

We promise to:

- continue in the apostles' teaching, in the breaking of bread, and in the prayers. We

vow to attend communal worship, participate in the sacraments, and pray—all as
ways to build and strengthen our relationship with God in Christ.

- persevere in resisting evil, and whenever
we fall into sin, repent and return to the
Lord. We recognize that baptism is not a
silver bullet solution for the problem of
human sin. A life lived in Christ requires
us to constantly admit when we are wrong,
ask forgiveness of God and one another,
and make amends, always seeking to do
better.

- proclaim by word and example the Good
News of God in Christ. An integral part
of the Christian life is proclamation. We
hope to live our lives in such a loving,
self-giving way that the story we tell of a
God who loves the world and gave Christ
to humanity unselfishly seems tangible
and real. So we promise to live so that the
words of our faith in Jesus ring true.

- seek and serve Christ in all persons, loving our neighbor as ourselves. These next
two questions follow from proclaiming
the Good News. How can we reflect the

unstinting love of God unless we love our neighbors as ourselves?

- strive for justice and peace among all people and respect the dignity of every human being. Justice, as Dr. Cornell West reminds us, is what love looks like in public.[10] We promise therefore not just to have friendly private feelings toward our fellow creatures of God, but to work for systems and institutions on this earth that create justice and peace for all God's children as a tangible outcome of that love.

To answer each question, the community responds that "we will, with God's help." There is no expectation that these promises can be accomplished perfectly through human will, but we do promise to try, and when we fail, to pick up and try again.

In essence, the Baptismal Covenant creates for us a road map of what it means to lead a daily life of faith. Like the Nicene Creed, it doesn't answer all

> In essence, the Baptismal Covenant creates for us a road map of what it means to lead a daily life of faith.

---

10 Cornell West, sermon given at Howard University, April 2011.

questions, nor does it require intellectual assent
to a series of propositions. What it does is ask
the baptized to commit to a way of living where
we make the reality of a loving God who dwells
with us in Christ visible through our actions and
choices in the world.

Eucharist

If baptism is the gateway sacrament, the Eucharist is the cornerstone sacrament—the one everything else is built upon. It is the one sacrament,
perhaps more than any other, that encapsulates
our relationship with God. Certainly it is the one
we experience the most frequently.

Chances are, this is what you've experienced
of the Episcopal Church. The Eucharist occupies the place of honor on Sunday mornings.
The current Book of Common Prayer declares it the
principle act of worship for
the gathered community—
the moment when the priest
takes bread and wine, prays
over them, and distributes
them to the gathered community as Christ's body and
blood for us.

Eucharist: a Greek
word literally meaning
thanksgiving, which
refers to the central sacrament of Christian worship–the blessing and
consuming of bread
and wine–which we understand to be participation in Christ himself.

Like baptism, the Eucharist is one of the oldest rituals we have. Scholars tell us that the earliest Christians celebrated a common meal with each other from the very beginning, and have been doing so ever since. We can trace the prayers we say to these earliest gatherings; the vestments and motions we use to the Byzantine and medieval church periods. This weekly devotion is ancient.

Yet what is it, exactly, that we are doing when we celebrate the Eucharist? Why the importance placed on this bit of bread and sip of wine?

For one thing, it is in the Eucharist that the pattern of the liturgy finds its shape. On the night he was betrayed, the synoptic[11] Gospels tell us that Christ took bread, gave thanks for it, blessed it, broke it, and gave it to his friends. This pattern is reflected in what we do on Sunday mornings. We gather together as a community. We hear the scriptures read and preached upon as we give thanks for our life together. We bless the bread and wine as we take them as communion, and finally we break apart again in order to go out and

---

11 *Synoptic* is a scholarly word that means "seen together." It refers to the Gospels of Matthew, Mark, and Luke, because they are so similar to each other.

be Christ's body in the world—ordinary people transformed into something holy. So the Eucharist gives us a pattern for what it means to live a Christian life: come together, pray, receive, and break apart to serve.

On a deeper level though, the Eucharist signals Christ's presence with us in a more direct and visceral way. In the Eucharist, we are reminded of Christ's death, resurrection, and ascension, as we rehearse the story of those earth-shaking events over again. But this isn't just nostalgia for a good story—as we recite these words, we are asking that we might enter into the life of Christ as we recount the events. We ask that we might become one with Christ in the Eucharist, as we ask the Holy Spirit to consecrate these simplest of things to our use. All this—so that we can go out of the church doors, ready and able to be the hands and feet of Christ in the world around us. The Eucharist, for Anglicans, is not an end unto itself—it is the means by which we enter again and again into the life of Christ until we are transformed fully by it. It is the way in which we gradually learn to be Christ-like ourselves.

As we participate in the rhythms of the Eucharist again and again, we are practicing a particular way of existing in the world—a way of both being Christ's people and of being Christ's body. We practice in our liturgy being the sort of people Christ calls us to be: self-giving, loving, attentive to God, to each other, and to the needs of the world. There is a real sense in which each celebration of the Eucharist becomes an outpost of God's reign on earth—an embassy of God's kingdom where we can be free to be citizens of heaven for a moment in time.

A practical note might be in order here: you might feel awkward or intimidated participating in the Eucharist for the first time. This is not something to stress over—there are many "right" ways to partake. Watching the person ahead of you for some guidance is usually a good idea. Generally speaking, people stretch out their hands, one palm over the other, in the basic shape of a cross, so that the priest may place a bit of bread there. Then you can either eat the bread, or wait to dip it in the cup of wine that comes around next. If the idea of a common cup makes you immediately envision the bubonic plague, don't worry about that either. The vast majority of Episcopal churches use port, or other fortified wine, that features a higher alcohol concentration than table wine. That alcohol, combined with the silver of the chalice, offer two natural germ-fighting measures that kill off most of anything that tries to jump from person to person. But if germs are a major concern for you, or if you cannot consume alcohol, know that receiving only the bread, or only the wine, counts as receiving the entire Eucharist.

The Other Sacraments: Ordination, Marriage, Reconciliation, Confirmation, Unction

Baptism and Eucharist are the two most common sacraments and are the two mentioned in the Gospels. However, the church also recognizes five other sacraments:

- *Confirmation*
  - ▷ Confirmation is the act of a bishop to accept a person's adult confirmation of faith. Particularly if they were baptized as an infant, confirmation is an opportunity for them to stand before the congregation and claim ownership of their faith for themselves.
  - ▷ The parallel rite to confirmation is reception, which is appropriate for those adults who wish to officially join the Episcopal Church, but who already made a public

confession of faith as adults in another denomination. The same rules apply: there
is some degree of preparation, the bishop
lays hands upon you and asks for the Holy
Spirit to sanctify your endeavors, etc. The
only difference is that the Episcopal Church
does not like to repeat sacraments already
performed elsewhere.

- *Ordination*
  - ▷ This is the setting aside of certain persons in
    order to empower and lead the church in its
    ministry—about which more will be said in
    the next chapter. It is how we create clergy.

- *Marriage*
  - ▷ A familiar rite to most, this is the joining
    together of two adults in a faithful commit-
    ted relationship, which the church believes
    symbolizes an aspect of Christ's love for
    humanity. This sacrament is unlike any
    other, in that here, it is the couple who per-
    form it, and the priest is only on hand to
    bless what they have accomplished. In the
    Episcopal Church, marriage is extended to
    any two adults in a committed, lifelong,
    and faithful relationship, with consent of
    clergy.

- *Reconciliation*
    - ▷ If you grew up in a Roman Catholic tradition, then this sacrament is more familiar to you under the name "Confession." The Episcopal Church practices it as well, but does not consider it mandatory in the same way. Instead, it is offered as a pastoral service for those who are especially burdened by guilt or shame and need counsel. Similar to the Roman Catholic practice, though, the seal of reconciliation is inviolable, and nothing that is said in that context may be repeated.
- *Unction*
    - ▷ This denotes the practice of anointing the sick and praying for their healing—a practice of the church that dates back to the times of the apostles. This sacrament includes anointing a person immediately prior to their death, but is not limited to such an extreme case. (So you should not be alarmed if a cleric shows up to pray with you prior to a routine surgery!)

A note: here in the early part of the twenty-first century, it might sound odd to speak of sacraments as being transformative. After all, we are modern people, possessing of solid beliefs in evolution, climate change, and iPhones. The thought that coming to church and taking a bit of consecrated bread on your tongue might change you sounds like nonsense.

But ours is also a world of symphonies, the Northern Lights, and vistas that take your breath away. Transcendence exists—in countless tiny miracles that surround us on a daily basis. I can't think of anyone I know who has not experienced transcendence at some point or another—from tearing up from realizing how much your child has grown, to the miraculous panic of falling in love. Sacraments are places where people have reliably found transcendence—an encounter with God—over the years. The church's delineation of sacraments does not discount the reality that God comes to us in many ways, and in

> Sacraments are places where people have reliably found transcendence–an encounter with God–over the years.

many experiences. These are just the places that people have sighted God more often than others. So the church continues to offer them in the hopes that we might find God with more ease.

Who's Who:
The People
in Your Parish

Assuming that you've wandered into your local Episcopal church to participate in a service,
then you've noticed the people standing in front,
wearing odd robes, leading the worship. These
friendly souls are clergy. Their roles are slightly
different in the Episcopal Church than in other
churches.

PRIEST

In nearly every Episcopal Church, you will find a priest. This is the person who stands in the front of the church and can be recognized by the collar around their neck, as well as either a elaborately decorated robe, called a *chasuble*, or a scarf, worn across both shoulders, called a *stole*.

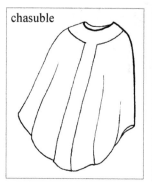
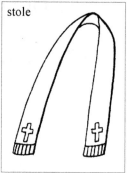

In the Episcopal Church, people of all genders can be priests. LGTBQ+ people can be priests. Young people, old people, black people, brown people, white people, disabled people, and marathon-running people can all be priests. Becoming a priest is based on God's call in a person's heart—not whatever physical abilities or characteristics they may possess.

However, being a priest also requires the person's community to recognize and confirm God's call to a person. In the same way that Boromir in the film adaptation of *The Fellowship of the Ring* warns that one cannot simply walk into Mordor, you cannot simply proclaim yourself a preacher and then set up your own Episcopal parish. Similar to the way we read scripture, much stock is placed in the community's discernment of call along with the individual's. The process of this joint discernment—individual and communal—prior to ordination takes several years and involves the bishop, the parish, physical and psychological evaluations, and most often a three-year course of study at a seminary. Such a lengthy and time-intensive process reflects the immense amount of trust and responsibility that the church will give to the ordained priest.

Once ordained, the priest may serve in a multitude of different ways: some priests serve as professors, some as chaplains, some as local parish priests, overseeing a congregation. The common thread between these disparate duties is the sacraments. In all professions they undertake, a priest's main duty is to perform and administer the sacraments for the people of God, as a sign of God's love for those among whom they live and work. Priests celebrate the Eucharist, bury the dead, baptize the new believers, bless, reconcile, and declare God's forgiveness. In all they do, and in how they exist in the world, a priest is to elevate earthly things, and make them holy, so that people may better catch a glimpse of the sublime presence of God.

Of course, all baptized people reflect the presence of God, but in ordination, we intentionally ask clergy to do this for us, to remind us what it looks like. Think of a baseball coach—a coach is someone who has the skills—someone who knows how to run, how to bunt, and how to field effectively, because they have done these things in their own lives. But now, that skilled person is dedicated to helping others perform these tasks as best they can. This is the job of a clergyperson.

A note here: nothing said so far should be taken to mean that clergy are intrinsically better than non-ordained people. Like baseball coaches, the clergy make mistakes and have flaws just like anyone else. Some clergy excel at listening at those in trouble, others have the bedside manner of Dr. Gregory House. Some clergy can preach the house down, others would put an insomniac to sleep. Some clergy went to their reward insisting God would never call women to the priesthood, others fight for full inclusion to this day. Ordination doesn't make a person perfect or give you a direct line to God; it gives you a job and a path to walk in the world. The individual's ability and willingness to carry those out is a separate matter.

DEACONS

Priests are not left to do their jobs alone. Deacons are another group of clergy who are ordained in a similar fashion. While priests are set aside to administer sacraments, deacons are set aside to minister to the world. In a sense, if priests are there to see to the needs of the church, the deacons are there to see to the outside world. Deacons often have specialized ministries outside the church, doing service work in various places like prisons, advocacy organizations, homeless shelters, domestic violence shelters, etc. They are the go-betweens of the institutional church and the secular world, making the faithful aware and alert to the needs of the most vulnerable.

In a liturgy, deacons can be spotted by their stoles draped over one shoulder (like a beauty contestant sash). They set up the vessels prior to the Eucharist, and they read the Gospel, if they are present.

BISHOPS

Bishops are the group of clergy from whence the Episcopal Church derives its name. The word in Greek for *bishop* is *episcope*, or "to oversee." A bishop, then, is one who oversees a section of the church—generally understood to be a geographic section.

The Episcopal Church is divided into geographic sections called *dioceses*, and a bishop oversees each one. Bishops are elected, and once installed, they remain the bishop for the rest of their life. (It's like being a Supreme Court justice.) Bishops travel around their diocese and visit their parishes to check in, perform confirmations, and ensure the welfare and well-being of their flock. In many ways, if we think of a priest like a baseball coach, a bishop is a general manager. The priest is on the ground, interacting with the team on a day-to-day basis. The bishop is slightly farther off, but is well-acquainted with how things are going, and is charged with the long-term vision and scope of the team.

Bishops can be spotted in a liturgy via the stick they carry, which resembles a shepherd's staff, and their pointy hats, called *miters*.

LAITY

The most important group of ministers in the church is not the clergy; it is the non-ordained people. These are the folk who give freely of their time and talent to serve in the church in various capacities.

It is the laypeople who do the hardest and truest work of the reign of God—both in the world during the week and in church on Sunday. Laypeople help make governing decisions for the church (more on that in a second), participate in the liturgy, proclaim the Good News, and carry out the work of the gospel. Within the liturgy, on a Sunday morning, you will see non-ordained folks reading the scripture, administering the sacramental wine, carrying crosses and torches in processions, showing people where to sit, making music, and doing all the various tasks that are needed to keep the church running.

WHO'S WHO: THE PEOPLE WHO RUN THE SHOW

Despite the pivotal role they might play during a liturgy, clergy are not in charge of the church. Mostly, we like to believe that Jesus is in charge of his church and is sending us the Spirit to guide us into all truth.

However, it still helps us to organize ourselves such that we can listen attentively to that Spirit and carry out her ideas, and for that, we need committees. Since 1789, the Episcopal Church, across the United States and beyond, has been governed by a structure called General Convention.

General Convention

The initial plans for a once-every-three-year convention of the entire church were first laid out by William White, in Philadelphia, and soon after, the first convention was called in 1789 at Christ Church, Philadelphia. Contrary to many popular stories, the structure of General Convention isn't really based on the structure of the (then) nascent Congress, but the two are not entirely dissimilar.

There are two distinct groups of General Convention: the House of Deputies and the House of Bishops. Any matter must be passed in identical form by both houses in order to take effect. The House of Bishops includes every living bishop within the church. The House of Deputies includes those elected out of each diocese across the church, with a maximum of four lay deputies and four clergy deputies from each diocese. All told, that is over eight hundred participants in the House's deliberations.

General Convention, when it meets every three years, considers such matters as the general church's budget, matters of policy, liturgy, music, and the internal rules for the church, known as canons. General Convention also has the ability to make changes to the prayer book. This is such a serious idea that any change to the official prayer book requires approval of two successive General Conventions in a row. Essentially, when General Convention meets, the whole Episcopal Church gathers in one place for two weeks of rejoicing, worship, long days, late nights, and deliberative discernment together—and it is in this gathering that the highest earthly authority in the Episcopal Church rests.

Vestry

While not nearly as large, the nearest parallel for the General Convention on a local level is the parish vestry. The parish priest is charged with overseeing the liturgy and the spiritual life of a congregation, but in all matters temporal, the vestry works with the local clergy. The vestry is composed of baptized, non-ordained adult members of the parish who are elected. It is the vestry that makes the decisions for the life of the parish: how the money is spent, what color the new carpet should be, whether to buy new hymnals, etc. All the day-to-day work of overseeing a typical nonprofit organization is the work of the vestry. The priest and vestry work together to keep the parish on track and make decisions for the good of all.

You

All this is to say, the church does not function without an immense amount of help from its members—people who care and have opinions and just want to help. There are dedicated folks who polish the silver. There are helpful souls who watch the babies in the nursery. There are quiet parishioners who speak up against injustice in the world and befriend the unfriendly in their workplace. There are hardworking individuals who make casseroles to take to those who are bereaved or recovering from a major surgery. No church can operate without the help and guidance of so many regular, normal people just like you.

Look at Where We Started

An Origin Story

To answer the existential question of how we got here requires two different answers.

In one sense, the Episcopal Church came from where all churches come from: a movement begun by the first followers of Jesus of Nazareth, who carried the good news of his resurrection around the ancient world. Eventually their movement gained such strength and power, despite considerable oppression and violence from the state, that it formed an institution and persisted through the rise and fall of empires, eventually becoming an empire unto itself.

That is the simple answer of how all Christian churches came to be. The followers of Jesus felt so passionately about him that they wanted to tell new people about him and so here we are. However, there are certain unique features of the Episcopal branch of that movement, and so that part of the story is where we now turn.

Once the church as an institution was established in the Roman Empire, it began to send out missionary expeditions throughout the known world, including to the then-uncharted British Isles. Augustine of Canterbury was sent from Rome to Britain and established the first church there in 597 CE. However, this did not mean the church was organized.

The church that grew up in Britain was separated from the Roman center of power by thousands of miles and a couple of boat rides—so it cultivated several unique strands of tradition apart from Rome.

Some of the differences were large, and some were small. Monasteries were more popular in England than the Continent, which relied on parish churches, bishops, and dioceses. British Christianity placed a greater emphasis on penance. The British used different liturgical colors, and even recognized a different date for Easter than did their Continental siblings. There were enough differences present that by the time they were squashed—by the papal reforms of Gregory the Great and better communication technology—the Christians in Great Britain had the distinct impression that they were definitely different from those in Europe.

This lingering sense of difference will come into play when Henry VIII ascends to the throne. Henry, we should note, initially was a big supporter of the Roman Church. He wrote a book attacking Martin Luther,[12] entitled *The Defence of the Seven Sacraments.* For his pains, the pope awarded him the title "Defender of the Faith" in 1521.[13]

However, Henry had some problems cropping up on the home front. Despite his best ef-

---

12 Martin Luther is the German monk who began the European Protestant Reformation by nailing 95 Theses on the door of a cathedral in Wittenberg.

13 This is a title that the British monarch still holds—though in Henry's case, it would prove fairly ironic.

forts, he could not seem to father a son by his wife, Catherine of Aragon, so the security of the throne was at risk. Also, he was rapidly running out of money because of various foreign wars and other bad decisions. It occurred to the devout Henry that possibly his bad luck was caused by the fact that Catherine had formerly been married to his brother—so Henry's marriage to her violated God's law and God was now punishing him. He asked the pope for an annulment of his marriage with Catherine.

The pope, however, knew that Catherine's nephew (now the Holy Roman Emperor) had previously invaded and sacked Rome, so he was loathe to irritate him (or his standing armies) again. He refused the annulment. A frustrated Henry convened Parliament to take matters into his own hands and forced through a law that declared the king, and not the pope, the Head of the Church in England in 1534. Thus was the Church of England established. Soon after, at the king's request and with little choice, the clergy of England granted him an annulment.

Initially, Henry was not interested in theological or liturgical reform. What he wanted was his annulment and access to the money that the

Roman Church had in England. Having gotten these, he basically lost interest in the whole project. However, Thomas Cranmer had been appointed by Henry to be the new archbishop of Canterbury,[14] and he had some ideas.

It was Cranmer, under Henry's successor Edward, who wrote the bulk of the first prayer book in English. Archbishop Cranmer began to put some of the Reformation ideas into practice largely on his own. He outlawed feast and fast days and began liturgies and Bible readings in English throughout the country—all of which were significant steps away from Roman Catholicism. The cadence of the prayer book that we take for granted comes from his writing, as he wrote the first editions of the Book of Common Prayer in 1549 and 1552.

However, it was not until the accession of Elizabeth I that Anglicanism came into its own. During the earlier reign of Mary, which saw the execution of Thomas Cranmer as a heretic in 1556, the Church of England reverted

---

14 Since the time of Augustine in the sixth century, the archbishop of Canterbury has been the highest rank in the church in England. When Henry severed ties with the pope, he also claimed the right to appoint someone to this position. Today, in 2019, the archbishop of Canterbury is Justin Welby.

to Roman Catholicism. But the change proved temporary; Elizabeth had a similar bent as her father and saw the virtues of leading an independent church.

At her request, the Cranmer prayer book was republished and achieved its final form in 1662.[15] She also ended the tug of war between the more stringent English Protestants and English Catholics with the Elizabethan Settlement, which decreed that the government did not care what a person privately believed, so long as they appeared at church and prayed in the authorized way—according to the Book of Common Prayer. Her court-appointed theologian, Richard Hooker, began to hammer out the Anglican method of theology, viewing scripture, tradition, and reason as the chief sources of authority. It was only under Elizabeth that the Church of England finally became a recognizable entity, with its own distinct voice and perspective.

Elizabeth also oversaw the beginning of En-

---

15 That's the form it is still in. It would take an Act of Parliament to change the Authorized Prayer Book in the UK, and as Parliament has many other things to worry about, it has not gotten around to it in lo, these many years.

glish expansion into the Western Hemisphere. When the first English colonists landed at what is now First Landing, Virginia, in 1607 and celebrated the Eucharist with their chaplain, Robert Hunt, they would end up establishing the seeds of the Episcopal Church, and what is now the worldwide family of churches known as the Anglican Communion.

A byproduct of colonization, the Anglican Church followed English exploration, springing up wherever England started a settlement. Because the American colonies were administered differently, the church took root in each new colony differently as well. In Virginia, New York, and Connecticut, where the colony was an official governmental endeavor, the Anglican Church was officially established. To hold office, government officials had to be a registered member of the local parish, and parishes received tax revenue as in England. In places like Massachusetts or Rhode Island, where the colony was established through a protest, or a differing religious community, the Anglican Church was slower to take root. (In Boston, the Anglican churches were so unpopular in that Puritan city that the parish had to bury their dead in the basement, so that mourning visitors would not be heckled and harassed when tending to the graves.)

Like the initial Christians in Britain, the Anglican Church grew up with profound cultural differences than its mother church in England. Due to a shortage of trained clergy, laypeople had considerably more power than they had back home and became adept at running parishes on their own. Because there was no feudal system to provide income for clergy, churches began to rent pews for income, or accept yearly pledges from their parishioners—even those that received government support. There was no bishop resident in the Colonies, so clergy, too, enjoyed more latitude than in England.

When the Revolutionary War came, the colonial church faced a conundrum: the majority of its clergy were British-trained and British-raised. The only authorized prayer book in use required daily prayers for the king and an oath of loyalty at ordination. Nearly half of the Anglican colonial community had either fled back to England or north to Canada by 1789. Could the Anglican Church survive without the crown for sustenance?

Different Anglicans tried to answer this question. William White wrote a pamphlet in 1782 arguing for the church to be divvied up into districts, each district having its own administrator. He thought the toddler-church should get its own bishops, since bishops had been central to Anglican understanding since the early days. American bishops, however, would not have the rights of lords or of governors, but be elected and oversee their diocese. The problem was how.

The churches in Connecticut thought White's idea was so great, they decided to try it. They elected Samuel Seabury to be the first bishop. Seabury headed over to England to receive his consecration, but discovered that no one would do the honors. The problem he encountered was one of loyalty: the accepted way to create a new bishop was to have three existing bishops lay hands upon the new bishop's head. This had been understood since the Council of Nicea. However, the ordination rite in the English prayer book required an allegiance oath to the king that the Americans had just rebelled against. As part of an established church, the English bishops were unwilling to participate in a ceremony that would not include this loyalty oath, to legitimize a church of rebels against the British throne.

Undeterred, Seabury headed to Scotland, where the Anglican Church and the clergy were quite comfortable no longer swearing oaths of allegiance in their ordinations. Three Scottish bishops ordained him, but asked that the new American church remember its debt to Scotland. Accordingly, from this act of friendship, the Episcopal Church got its name—borrowing from the Scottish Episcopal Church—and its shield— borrowing from the flag of St. Andrew's, as well as its first bishop.

And so was born this new creature that called itself The Episcopal Church. In the ensuing years, it would face expansion and decline, fights about slavery, civil rights, women's rights, and prayer book revision. It would spread into over fourteen countries, following in the wake of American military expansion. But the elements it started with—a respect for the entire community gathered; a belief in scripture, tradition, and reason; and some degree of comfort with the unknown—would continue to serve it in the coming years.

ORIGIN STORY, PART 2:
AMERICAN BOOGALOO

Once the American church had sorted out What To Do About Bishops, it then turned its attention to being the Establishment without actually being established. For much of its early history, the Episcopal Church in the United States was content to sedately establish parishes as it had members and provide for the spiritual needs of whoever wandered through its doors. The furor of the Great Awakening and the various revival movements of early America largely left the Episcopal Church to the wayside, and it wasn't until the early nineteenth century that a few bishops suggested that the church might want to expand westward. If it wasn't too much trouble.

So to the west went the church, encouraged by bishops such as Jackson Kemper and Philander Chase. Missionary societies within the church were set up, and as the American presence began to spread around the world via trade and other manifest-destiny related endeavors, so too did the Episcopal presence.

At the same time, even as the church braved new frontiers, the old, besetting sins of the American experiment still persisted. The record of the Episcopal Church toward black people, both free and enslaved, is mixed, at best.

On the one hand, the theology was clear: in the eyes of God, baptism made everyone, regardless of race, equal in the sight of God. On the other hand, Episcopalians of the time, and the church as a whole, had a very difficult time pushing against a society that was built on, and enforced, white supremacy.

So while the church took pains to evangelize and baptize people of all races, it had a hard time creating a welcoming space after the water had dried. In the mid-eighteenth century, Richard Allen and Absalom Jones, two lay preachers in Philadelphia, had such success evangelizing their fellow former slaves, that it alarmed the white leadership of St. George's Methodist Church. Upon arriving at worship one morning and discovering that the leadership intended to segregate the worship space, Allen and Jones left and never looked back. Absalom Jones took his group of worshippers and founded St. Thomas African Episcopal Church, the first black Episcopal Church in the country in the 1790s, and ultimately pursued ordination as a priest, becoming also the first black Episcopal priest. However, the bishop of Pennsylvania never allowed the parish access to the diocesan convention, or allowed Jones voting rights at clerical council.[16]

Similarly, during the Civil War, the Episcopal Church as a whole could not make up its mind about what side it was on. There were many clergy, especially in the North, who opposed slavery on moral and theological grounds. And yet, because of the staunch, pro-Confederacy stance of many Southern clergy, the church never took an official stance with regards to slavery. All other Protestant denominations ultimately split as a result of the Civil War and the rending of the country. The Episcopal Church did not. Following the war, the Southern dioceses returned to General Convention, one by one, as if nothing had happened.

This failure to take a stand on the evil of slavery would reverberate through history. In the years following the war, the Episcopal Church

---

16 I would be remiss if I did not include praise here for the online exhibit at the Episcopal Archives regarding the history of African Americans in the church. It is incredibly thorough, absorbing, and much more in-depth than it is possible to be in such a brief volume as this. Their exhibit on Native Americans and the church is also excellent.

continued to be of many minds when it came to race relations. In parts of the church, all people were afforded access to the ordination process; in other parts, black people were forbidden. In some Southern dioceses, segregation was the order of the day, and in other places, integration was encouraged. Like the situation prior to the war, the church leaders had a difficult time taking a moral stand on issues that might cause division in the church.

However, ministry continued, moral muddles aside. People like James Solomon Russell and Anna Alexander were not dissuaded by the institutional church's confusion and did incredible work. The Rev. James Solomon Russell traveled on horseback all over rural southern Virginia at the turn of the twentieth century and founded thirty-seven parishes, as well as St. Paul's College in Lawrenceville, Virginia—all for black people now emerging from slavery. He was elected suffragan bishop of Alabama and North Carolina, but refused both elections in order to continue his ministry to the people of Virginia.

Deacon Anna Alexander followed a similar path in Georgia. She was the only black woman ever ordained as a deaconess. After receiving her education as a teacher from St. Paul's College in Virginia, she returned to Georgia and spent her lifetime educating black children—often with no money or resources to draw on. One year, during the Depression, only two of her thirty students could afford to pay the nickel fee for schooling. However, she persevered and taught generations of children the gospel.

As the Episcopal Church entered the twentieth century, several streams were merging at once. On the one hand, the old, established church of the coastal colonies was still very much in evidence. Figures like Teddy and Franklin Roosevelt, the Vanderbilts, and J. P. Morgan connected the church with the upper crust, the establishment, and as close to American nobility as one could get.

On the other hand, even as these figures maintained the image of the Episcopal Church as staid, solid, and upper class, the Oxford movement crossed the ocean from England and found a welcome home in America's melting pot. The Oxford movement emphasized prayer and proper liturgy, as well as the doctrine of the Incarnation. God became human, and therefore this material world we inhabit as humans must be valued, cherished, and used to reach the divine.

However, within the Oxford movement, many discovered a specific critique of the rapidly modernizing world. God became human, so humans must be infinitely lovable by God—did God really want his beloved to dwell in slums? To die of hunger on the streets? Did God want his beloved to work without ceasing in dangerous factories? What would the Incarnate God have to say about income inequality?

In the United States, this increased awareness gave impetus to reforming figures, who coupled the privilege with the established church with empathy and zeal. Frances Perkins, Franklin Roosevelt's Secretary of Labor, was a devout Episcopalian who credited her faith with spurring her to create Medicaid, Social Security, and many of the labor safeguards we enjoy today. Many other prominent Episcopalians worked to assist the waves of immigrants, alleviate poverty, and safeguard working people.

By the middle of the twentieth century, women, as well as African Americans, were pushing for greater roles in the institutional church. The struggle for greater African American inclusion had been going on since the founding of the country, but moved into a higher gear with the advent of the modern civil rights movement. As the wider world reckoned with the hypocrisy inherent in the promises made in its founding documents and the realities of Jim Crow, the church also had to take an inward look at how it treated its historically black churches and black clergy. Many Episcopal clergy—black and white—joined the civil rights movement. The seminarian Jonathan Myrick Daniels joined the Freedom Riders in Alabama and was killed while protecting seventeen-year-old Ruby Sales. It was Episcopalian Thurgood Marshall in *Brown v. Board of Education* who successfully argued before the Supreme Court that segregation was unconstitutional. He was later appointed a justice to the Supreme Court under President Johnson.

It was during this time that the church first started to take a strong political stand on racism and segregation, largely led by figures like the Rt. Rev. John Hines. A lifelong Southerner, and elected presiding bishop after being the bishop in Texas, Bishop Hines was also a student of the Social Gospel. He believed that Christians had a unique obligation to side with the poor, the downtrodden, and the oppressed—and that this presently included racial minorities and women. In the immediate wake of the assassination of the Rev. Dr. Martin Luther King Jr, Hines asked the General Convention to reorganize its financial priorities, initiating what was termed the "Special Program." This program would use the wealth of the church to give impoverished and struggling inner-city groups financial assistance—with no strings attached. Hines then called a special meeting of General Convention to deal specifically with this new program. (Only one other special meeting of the convention had ever been called in the history of the Episcopal Church, so this was a major deal.) Adding to the significance, Hines increased the delegate count, intentionally including youth, women, and people of color at the convention for the first time.

In many ways, the special convention was a watershed moment in the Episcopal Church. It was a contentious meeting, made more complicated by the fact that Hines had made the classic mistake of failing to ask his own black Episcopal community for their input, and instead invited in outside groups. This fueled mistrust and miscommunication, which further alienated the already distrustful conservative wing of the church. The end result was a decision to raise an additional $200,000 for the National Committee of Black Churchmen.[17]

However, for the first time, the church prioritized outreach for the benefit of the world, rather than to preserve its own establishment. It also began to see women, youth, and people of color as necessary voices in the discussion. And these were steps that could not be taken back. Even after Hines was succeeded in the 1970s by the Rt. Rev. John Maury Allin, who was widely perceived as a conservative—the church continued to give widely for alleviation of poverty, and allowed the ordination of women in 1976, even over Allin's own objections.

In some ways, the story of women's struggle in the church is both a much shorter one and in other ways, a much longer one. While women had been permitted to be unpaid deaconesses within the Episcopal Church since 1885, they were never allowed to serve in a liturgical role. Instead, deaconesses were sent out as mission-

---

17 According to https://www.episcopalarchives.org/ church-awakens/exhibits/show/specialgc/specialgc.

aries and workers, teaching school, setting up hospitals, and doing the hard work of service. (Recall, Anna Alexander was a deaconess.) Over the course of 1885 to 1970, there were approximately five hundred deaconesses.[18] This was not the only role women had, of course.

Throughout the nineteenth century, women also organized, funded, and carried out the majority of the missionary work of the Episcopal Church, despite not actually being allowed to serve on the actual Board of Missions.[19] Recognizing that this was the height of silliness, the Rt. Rev. Horatio Potter of New York suggested that the women should actually get their own committee, and in 1871, the Women's Auxiliary was born.[20] (Note: it was the Women's Aux-

---

18 See https://www.episcopalchurch.org/library/glossary/deaconess.

19 This is true! In fact, more women have served as missionaries in the history of the church then men. For more on this, I commend the history of the UTO, which is available on their website (https://unitedthankoffering.com/about-uto/history/) The fundraising that the Women's Auxillary carried out coalesced into the United Thank Offering, which still exists.

20 Mary Sudman Donovan, "Zealous Evangelists: The Women's Auxiliary to the Board of Missions," *Historical Magazine of the Protestant Episcopal Church* 51, no. 4 (1982): 371–83.

illary to the Board of Missions—not to the entire church.) It effectively brought together all the local women's groups that had been organizing missionary work up until now, and by 1882, the Women's Auxillary was the primary funder for twenty-nine missionary bishops: seven foreign and twenty-two domestic.[21] (See? They were not messing around.)

The work of the Women's Auxiliary continued to flourish—so much, in fact, that the rest of the institutional church began to look to it for supplemental funding—a turn which was not all that popular with the women, who still were not allowed to sit on vestries, serve as deputies to General Convention, or have any liturgical role at all. Following a major church restructuring in 1919, when General Convention combined the Board of Missions, the Board of Religious Education, and the Commission of Social Service into one organization under a National Council, the Women's Auxillary now found itself funding the entire church-wide agenda—yet without representation in setting the agenda.

---

21 Ibid.

Not unrelated to this, the clamor grew for women to be treated as equal lay members of the church—with full rights to sit on vestries and at Convention. As early as 1913, Bishop Benjamin Brewster of Maine tried to amend the constitution to give full rights to female communicants; the matter was squashed in committee. In 1919, the House of Bishops again discussed letting a committee decide what to do about giving women equal rights within the church, but ultimately decided that it would be "inexpedient," adding however their deepest appreciation for the work of women.[22]

In 1946, the Diocese of Missouri decided to sally forth and elect a woman as a deputy to General Convention. Consequently, Mrs. Elizabeth Dyer appeared at Convention that year and asked to be seated. This confounded everyone, until someone pointed out that the language in the canons was not gender-specific, referring instead to "any layman may stand for election." This move succeeded, and Mrs. Dyer was able to represent Missouri. However, during the same convention,

---

22 https://www.episcopalarchives.org/house-of-deputies/women/delegates.

the Committee on Amendments released a report arguing that "layman" in the canons refers to the male gender only. A proposed amendment to remove the gender-specific language from the canons was defeated by only seven votes. It would be several more decades before women could return to the floor.

Absolutely no one was sitting still in the interim, however. As the General Convention of 1946 was trying to figure out what to do with Elizabeth Dyer, the Women's Auxillary was also meeting, literally across the street.[23] They heard about the kerfuffle and sent a telegram across the street, asking the Convention to interpret "layman" inclusively. This did not work.

Undeterred, many dioceses now figured they might as well elect women as deputies and just see what happened, since it worked with Elizabeth Dyer. However, thanks to the ruling by the Committee of Amendments, these deputies were not seated in 1949, 1951, etc., even after public opinion began to soften.

In 1964, Presiding Bishop Arthur Lichtenberger even went so far as to sweetly rebuke Gen-

---

23 Remember them? They have all the money!

eral Convention, telling them in most Episcopal fashion that their "unwillingness to face the fact that women are . . . of the laity and members of the Body of Christ" was regrettable. In 1967, the constitutional amendment was passed for the first time, and in 1970, women deputies were seated at long last. (Please note—women were allowed to sit on vestries in 1964.[24])

As soon as women formally joined General Convention, the movement toward ordination began again in earnest. It was proposed immediately in 1970, and only defeated narrowly in 1973. However, by this time, dioceses had sent women to seminary and ordained them to the diaconate, and the growing consensus was any continued delay was unjust. In July 1974, eleven women were ordained to the priesthood in Philadelphia, so the issue was forced. This time, the measure passed, and all orders of ministry were opened to women at long last.

As the church moved into the twenty-first century, the inclusivity with which the church had learned to approach all God's children slow-

---

24 https://www.episcopalarchives.org/house-of-deputies/women/delegates.

ly spread to the LGBTQ community. Unlike the struggles of women and people of color within the church, there had always been gay and lesbian people in nearly every level of the church. What began to change, however, was the openness with which this was acknowledged, and how the church addressed the needs of this community.

In 1974, Louie Crew founded Integrity, after visiting the famously progressive Grace Cathedral in San Francisco, hoping to meet other gay Christians, and being turned away. Organizing around the principle that God gave everyone— gay and straight alike—the gift of sexuality, intending that it be used in healthy, life-giving ways, Integrity grew quickly, and at the first national convention in 1975, it had two hundred members.

Immediately, Integrity began to push for recognition and equal rights to the ordination process for LGBTQ people within the church. In 1976, the church officially prohibited discrimination against gays and lesbians within the church. With the advent of the AIDS crisis in the 1980s, the Episcopal Church was one of the first American denominations to respond. Particularly in urban areas that were hardest hit, like New York City,

San Francisco, and Atlanta, it was Episcopal parishes that first organized hospices, food drives, and other ways to support those affected. These responses helped change public opinion in large areas of the church. In 1985, prompted by Integrity, the church passed a General Convention resolution that denounced the view that AIDS was a divine punishment and instead described it as a public health crisis the church needed to address.

Ordination, however, was a more complex matter. While some bishops had been quietly ordaining gay men for a long time, other bishops were firmly against it. In 1979, the House of Bishops had passed a resolution saying that ordaining gay clergy was "not appropriate," though because House of Bishops' statements usually don't have the force of law, and because the language of this one was unusually polite, it did not succeed in restraining anyone.

The issue came to a head in 1996, when the retired bishop of Iowa, the Rt. Rev. Walter Righter, was accused of heresy for ordaining an openly gay man to the diaconate. The court of bishops essentially had to decide if the Episcopal Church had any rules that definitely prohibited ordination on the basis of sexuality. It turned out the

Episcopal Church did not, and Bishop Righter was cleared of all charges. To clarify matters, soon after General Convention affirmed that gay, lesbian, and bisexual people could not be denied ordination on that basis alone.

In ensuing years, the Rt. Rev. V. Gene Robinson was elected bishop of New Hampshire, becoming the first openly gay bishop. Same-gender marriage liturgies were written and put into use throughout the Episcopal Church, and as civil law finally recognized the right to marriage for all people, the Episcopal Church was there at the forefront of the movement.

At the present moment, our challenge remains how to serve the world that God has given us in the midst of the challenges that surround us. How can we ensure that all voices are heard and heeded, even and especially the ones we must learn to listen for? How can we ensure that the blessings of the church are open to all people? And how can we ensure that the legacy that has been passed into our hands will be safe to be handed on to future generations?

It is easy to see history, particularly church history, as a series of arguments where none should exist. It can be easy to conceive of church people as pedantic and focused on things that don't really matter, while great problems loom just outside their doors. However, the constant thread in the history of the Episcopal Church in the United States appears to me to be a group of people trying their hardest to do the will of the Spirit and to love each other—even as they get it wrong and get frustrated with each other. The twin commitments to follow the way of Jesus in this world and to love deeply the world that God gives us has led the church in some awkward places, some surprising turns, and some roller-coaster rides. But always, always, the people of the church have tried to follow their Christ, and to hold on to each other.

But What About . . . ?
FAQs

1. *What does the Episcopal Church believe
about gay rights?*

   The Episcopal Church, since the mid-1970s,
   has affirmed the innate worth and dignity of
   LGTBQ people through legislation at General
   Convention. This journey toward full inclusion reached a pivotal moment in 2003, when
   New Hampshire elected and consecrated the
   first openly gay bishop, V. Gene Robinson.
   Since then, the church has affirmed access to
   ordination for all people, regardless of gender

identity or sexual orientation. The church has allowed same-gender marriage liturgies since 2006, and in 2015, required that all bishops allow marriage to be accessible to all people throughout the church.[25]

Generally, the church teaches that to be LGBTQ is morally no different than to be straight, and is no way inherently sinful. Sexuality is like all other aspects of our human condition— it can be used either for good or bad purpose.

While it is overly optimistic to say that this stance extends to all local parishes, all across the reach of the United States, the overall stance of the Episcopal Church is emphatically accepting and affirming of LGBTQ people and their allies.

2. *What does the Episcopal Church believe about feminism?*

Similar to our story on gay rights, the Episcopal journey on feminism has been full of twists and turns. Beginning in the mid-1960s, women were first allowed to serve on ves-

---

25 https://www.episcopalchurch.org/lgbtq-church.

tries and as deputies at General Convention in 1970. In 1974, merely ten years later, eleven women were ordained in Philadelphia's Church of the Advocate by a few brave bishops in defiance of the refusal of General Convention to allow them to be ordained. In 1976, General Convention decided to "regularize" that ordination, and women were admitted to the priesthood. In 1989, Barbara Harris was elected bishop in Massachusetts, thus becoming the first woman elected bishop, and in 2009, the Rt. Rev. Katharine Jefferts-Schori was elected presiding bishop, setting another milestone.

The Episcopal Church does not teach complementarianism or similar theologies that would sort men and women into strict, predetermined, gender-assigned roles.

Again, like our path on gay rights, and like the rest of the country, while the overall stance of the church reflects openness and progress, we still have a ways to go to make the dream of an equal-access church a reality.

3. *How much of the Nicene Creed do I HAVE to believe?*

Good news! No one will quiz you!

This is up to you. Part of the residue of the Elizabethan Settlement is that Episcopalians are extremely comfortable with individual diversity when it comes to how we think of the prayers we say. The person standing beside you may really be struggling with the resurrection part, having just suffered a loss. The person in front may be really furious with the institutional church and not want to talk about that part. Someone else may not want to commit to forgiveness, being in the middle of a fight with a family member. It is to be expected, and even celebrated, that this sort of variety of belief exists in a congregation. (If everyone believes the same, that's not a congregation; that's a cult. Back away and call a trusted adult.)

Belonging to a faith community involves acknowledging that you, because of the influence of these different believers around you, may grow and change. You will probably believe differently because of their influence and they, because of you. That's good. We teach

each other. So when we say the creed, we say it together, regardless of whether we are 100 percent sold on a given line on that given day, because it reflects our commitment to THIS faith community, and to our willingness to journey with them. Who knows? There may come a day when you grow into a committed love of the entire creed. Or you may discover that you see it as a poetic rendition of the faith of ages. Or something entirely different. Either way, it is a symbol of our commitment to each other and the saints that came before us.

4. *There are days I don't know that God exists. Is that OK?*

Perfectly fine. If you were beyond a doubt convinced of the existence of God every moment of your life, I would be a trifle concerned. The opposite of faith is not doubt; it is certainty. The practice of doubting, of questioning in a faithful way can actually deepen your faith. If you can find a trusted person or faith leader who will sit with you in your questions, you may find that your doubts lead you to a deeper connection to the Christ, who questioned a lot of things during his life. As Simone Weil wrote: "Christ likes us to prefer truth to Him because, before being Christ, He is truth. If one turns aside from Him to go toward the truth, one will not go far before falling into His arms."[26]

5. *I was baptized or confirmed when I was younger, but that priest did A Horrible Thing/was A Horrible Person. Do I need to get rebaptized?*

Believe it or not, this has been a concern for as long as the church has existed! It's a strange sort of comfort to realize that clergy have been misbehaving and dragging the institutional church into an existential crisis since day 2 of its existence.

The early church decided that the evil actions of an individual clergyperson DO NOT invalidate a sacrament they perform. (To claim otherwise is an official heresy, as noted at the Ecumenical Council of Nicea, circa 315.) Because a sacrament is an action of God, it is not dependent on that clergyperson's good char-

---

26 Simone Weil, *Waiting for God* (New York: HarperCollins, 1951), 27.

acter. God always acts through flawed matter—really, it's just a question of how flawed.

If, though, you are feeling continued effects from a spiritual leader who abused your trust, or caused you pain, please reach out to someone who can counsel you—either a therapist or a different faith leader. While the sacrament remains effective, and nothing can remove you from the love of God, frequently we need someone to remind us of that reality, especially when our trust has been abused.

6. *What do I wear to church?*

Honestly? Anything. Some congregations go all-out for the fancy clothes; some keep it very casual. More often, nowadays, you'll find a wide variety of clothing choices among the different folks who show up. But whatever you wear, you should not be turned away because of your sartorial choices.

7. *What about my kids?*

Chances are, the Episcopal Church you choose has some sort of program for kids—either a nursery for very small children, or a Sunday school program. However, you should feel free to keep your kids with you in church. Worship is for everyone: not just people who can follow along, or those who understand all the words, or who know all the theology. It might feel counterintuitive if your kids are younger, and on the squirmy side, but I have found that children do better in church the more they can see what's going on, so you might consider sitting up front. Because Episcopal worship is so interactive and sensory based, there is a lot to pay attention to! Colors, music, words to read, words to listen to, smells, bells—all sorts of things! You might be surprised at what your children notice and absorb.

Also, once a person is baptized, even if that baptism occurs when they are an infant, that person is a full member of the church and can fully participate. This means your baptized child can receive communion, as well as participate to the best of their ability: acolyte, serve on the altar guild, be an usher, be a reader, etc. If your child has an interest, it might be worth pursuing with your friendly neighborhood priest.

8. *What on earth is that priest wearing?*
   A poncho?

   Clergy, and others who have special jobs
   during the worship service, wear special
   clothes called vestments. The purpose of
   these is to take the focus off of the individual person and focus the congregation's attention on God. The vestments usually look the
   same, conveying humanity's equality before
   God. They also frequently blend in with the
   hangings in the front of the church, so that the
   leaders of the liturgy appear to literally fade
   into the wallpaper, rather than become the focus of attention.

9. *OK, I hear what you're saying. But I*
   still have some questions!

   Fantastic! I recommend you locate your
   friendly, local Episcopal priest and pepper
   them with your queries. Many of us clergy
   will even buy you coffee.

Further Reading

On Christian History:

Justo Gonzalez. *The Story of Christianity*. New York: HarperOne, 2014.

On Episcopal Church/Anglican History in particular:

Thomas Ferguson, *The Episcopal Story: Birth and* Rebirth. New York: Church Publishing, 2015.

On particular aspects of Episcopal History (black history in the Church, women's rights in the Church, etc.)

Episcopal Archives, https://www.episcopalarchives.org/.

Liturgical Theology:

James Farwell, *The Liturgy Explained.* New York: Morehouse, 2013.

Leonel Mitchell, *Praying Shapes Believing: A Theological Commentary on the Book of Common Prayer.* Updated by Ruth Meyers. New York: Seabury Books, 2016.

Welcome to . . .

Designed for the visitor, newcomer, or long-time member, *Welcome to a Life of Faith* in the Episcopal Church joins a series of books intended to make the Episcopal Church, its liturgy, and its practices fully accessible. Each book is conversational in tone and can be used individually or in small group settings.

Discover the full set at churchpublishing.org or wherever books are sold:

Welcome to Sunday: An Introduction to Worship in the Episcopal Church by Christopher Webber, ISBN 9780819219152

Welcome to the Bible by Vicki K. Black and Peter Wenner, ISBN 9780819219152

Welcome to the Episcopal Church: An Introduction to its History, Faith, and Worship by Christopher Webber, ISBN 9780819218209

Welcome to the Book of Common Prayer by Vicki K. Black, ISBN 9780819221308

Welcome to the Church Year: An Introduction to the Seasons of the Episcopal Church by Vicki K. Black, ISBN 9780819219664

Welcome to Anglican Spiritual Traditions by Vicki K. Black, ISBN 9780819223685

Welcome to Church Music and the Hymnal 1982 by Matthew Hoch, ISBN 9780819229427

Welcome to the Christian Faith by Christopher Webber, ISBN 780819227430

CPSIA information can be obtained
at www.ICGtesting.com
Printed in the USA
JSHW010906210223
37710JS00018B/19